W9-CJG-921

FAITH
IN FRIENDSHIP

My Friend Is
Muslim

by Khadija Ejaz

PURPLE TOAD
PUBLISHING

FAITH
IN FRIENDSHIP

My Friend Is Buddhist
My Friend Is Christian
My Friend Is Hindu
My Friend Is Jewish
My Friend Is Muslim

Printing 2   3   4   5   6   7   8   9

Publisher's Cataloging-in-Publication Data
Ejaz, Khadija
    Faith in friendship : my friend is Muslim / Khadija Ejaz
        p. cm.
Includes bibliographic references and index.
ISBN: 9781624690969
1. Islam – History – Juvenile literature. 2. Islam – Customs and practices – Juvenile literature.   I. Title.
 BP174
 297E
                                                        2014941906

eBook ISBN: 9781624690976

To my younger self, still out there in the past trying to stay afloat in post-9/11 America.— **Khadija Ejaz**

Contents

Muslims, like this young girl, always treat the Quran with great respect.

Ramadan With the Reeds

We have indeed revealed this (Message) in the Night of Power;
And what will explain to you what the Night of Power is?
The Night of Power is better than a thousand months.
Therein come down the angels and the Spirit by Allah's permission, on every errand;
Peace, until the rise of the morn.[1]

Nancy's eyes widened with wonder. "So you're saying that there are angels around us right now?"

I looked up from my copy of the English translation of the Holy Quran and nodded at my friend. "That's what the Quran says."

Nancy hugged herself and looked about my room from where we were sitting on my bed. She was squinting and trying to imagine the angels of Allah around us, but I knew she wouldn't be able to see them. Angels are made of light, and humans can't see them. We also can't see the *jinn*, whom Allah made from smokeless fire. The *jinn* are like human beings—some are good, some are bad, and they have families and religions of their own—but they live longer and travel faster.

"Give up, Nancy!" I laughed.

Nancy Winters is my best friend. We both attend seventh grade at the Queeny Public School here in St. Louis, Missouri. Our teacher, Miss Finney, found out that the Islamic festival of *Eid al-Fitr* was coming up, and she asked me to make a presentation about it to our class. Nancy volunteered to help me. She is spending the weekend with me at my home so we can work on the project together.

Nancy gave up on spotting an angel. She turned to me again. "Tell me more about 'The Night of Power.'"

"It's supposed to be the night that the Quran was first revealed to the world by Allah through the Prophet Muhammad, peace be upon him. No one knows which night it was, but most people believe that it was one of the last few nights of the Islamic month of Ramadan. You know, the month of fasting. We're in the last week of Ramadan right now. In Arabic, 'The Night of Power' is called *Laylat al-Qadr*."[2]

Nancy's eyes lit up.

"Hey, did I just hear your name in there somewhere?"

"Yes, you did." I told her that my name—Layla—is Arabic for "night." My parents chose that name for me because of my dark eyes and hair. My father, Hamza Reed, is an advertising executive. My mother, Mariam Akhmetova, owns an Islamic store here in St. Louis.

"Why did your mother not change her last name when she got married?"

I shrugged. "I've asked her about that before. She told me that it's not the usual Islamic tradition. Muslim women generally keep their names after marriage."

Nancy suddenly turned her head. "Hey, what's that sound?"

"That's the *adhaan*," I said. My father had installed software on his computer that played out the Islamic call to prayer for each of the five daily prayers. The software let us know the exact time of the evening prayer so that we could open our fasts on time.

I closed the Quran, kissed it, and carefully placed it on my bedside table. "Let's go to the dining room," I said. "It's *iftaari* time. Time to open our fast!"

My parents and my little sister, Zoha, were already in the dining room by the time Nancy and I showed up. Zoha is seven years old and has light brown hair and hazel eyes. She looks more like my mom. My older brother, Sinaan, is fifteen years old and has dark hair and eyes like our father.

"Where is Sinaan?" I asked my parents. The *adhaan* was still playing.

"He's outside with his friends," said my mother. She was opening a new package of dates. My father was pouring orange juice for all of us. "I'll give

This picture of my mother and father hangs in our living room. While Muslim homes may have photographs on display, religious places almost never have images of people or animals. Instead, they are decorated with geometric and floral designs and calligraphy (artistic writing).

him a call," he said. He pulled out his cell phone and gave Sinaan a ring. "Come home quickly, son; it's time to open your fast," he told him.

I heard our front door open and the sound of quick, heavy footsteps. A moment later, Sinaan was in the dining room with a couple of his friends. Hussein was born in America but his parents are from Malaysia; Ishaan and his family moved to the United States from India three years ago. Hussein is a Muslim and Ishaan is a Hindu, but my parents always keep our house open to our friends, especially during Ramadan.

"Ew, you're sweaty!" I said to Sinaan. He poked me on my waist and made me jump. "We were playing basketball," he said as he sat down at his usual place at the table. Hussein and Ishaan sat down next to him. Zoha was clambering onto her chair, and I had Nancy sit next to me.

The table was full of food—chunks of icy, red watermelon; a bowl full of shiny, green grapes; falafel; pieces of pita bread with hummus and garlic sauce; and of course, dates. *Subhan Allah* ("glorious is Allah")! My parents took their seats at the table, and we all took one date each. Nancy did too. My mother looked at her and smiled.

My family likes to open our fasts with fresh fruit and bread. What a delicious spread!

A Muslim family prays together before a meal.

"We're going to open our fast with a short Arabic prayer, Nancy," she said. "You may join in if you like. Everyone repeat after me."

Allahumma inni laka sumtu wa bika aamantu wa 'alayka tawakkaltu wa 'ala rizq-ika aftarthu.

We all began to eat our dates. "What did that prayer mean?" Nancy asked my mother. My mother replied, "It means, 'Oh Allah, I fasted for You, and I believe in You, and I break my fast with your sustenance.' We will now have a light meal before going off to quickly say our evening prayers. We shall have dinner when we are done praying. After that, it will be time for the *tarawih,* which is the night-time Ramadan prayer."

Little Zoha perked up from where she sat at the table. "Mommy," she said. "What are we having for dinner?"

"Fried chicken! Can you believe that new restaurant I told you about

serves zabiha meat?" Zabiha meat is prepared according to the laws of the Quran.

Sinaan shouted in delight and high-fived his friends. Our family always has trouble finding stores and restaurants that serve the kind of meat that Muslims can eat. Maybe this was our Ramadan miracle.

I turned to look at Nancy. She had never been to my house during Ramadan before. I wondered if she was comfortable.

"Do you like the falafel?" I asked her.

Nancy smiled at me. "Yes, I do. Thank you, Layla." She took a sip of her orange juice. "I am having so much fun with your family." She turned to look at my parents, my sister, my brother, and his friends, all of them talking to each other and enjoying the *iftaari* food. The *adhaan* had stopped playing on my father's computer, but the evening had just begun.

"Your family is so different," Nancy continued. "Your mother is a white woman from Russia, your father is a black man from America, but they are both Muslim. I can't wait to learn all about the religion that brought them together!"

...a white has no superiority over a black, nor does a black have any superiority over a white; [none have superiority over another] except by piety and good action. – Prophet Muhammad

The Muslim World

Some people think Muslims and Arabs are the same or that all Muslims are Arabs. In reality, they are two different things. A Muslim is someone who follows the religion of Islam. An Arab is a person whose native language is Arabic or who can trace his or her roots to an Arabic-speaking country.

Arabic has much in common with languages like Hebrew and Aramaic—they all originated in the Middle East and are grouped together under the family of Semitic languages. The Arabs, therefore, are a Semitic people like the Jews. Most Arab countries are located on the Arabian Peninsula and in Africa, and they are members of a regional group called the Arab League. Not all Arabs are Muslim, however; many are Jewish and Christian. Not all Muslims are Arab either.

The Muslim world spreads out beyond the Arab world and includes countries where Islam is practiced. There are 1.6 billion Muslims in the world. That's about one-fifth of the world's population, which makes Islam the second-most popular religion in the world after Christianity.[3]

Almost two-thirds of the world's Muslims live in the Asia-Pacific region.[4] Indonesia has the highest number of Muslims in the world. India and Pakistan have the next largest Muslim populations. In fact, there are more Muslims in those two countries than in the Middle East and North Africa combined.[5] Countries like Russia and China also have large Muslim populations, as do many countries in Europe and the Americas.

A Chinese Muslim boy

My Islamic school library has many books like these.

A Prophet From Mecca

"Layla, none of these books have pictures of the Prophet Muhammad, peace be upon him."

Masha Allah ("Allah wills it"), Nancy learns fast. She made sure she said "peace be upon him" every time she said the Prophet's name.

It was a quiet Saturday afternoon, and we were at the Islamic school. I go there every Sunday to learn about Islam. My brother and sister take classes there as well.

Nancy and I were sitting together inside the school's library. We had found many books about Islam and had laid them out in front of us on a table.

"You'll never find his picture anywhere," I said. "Muslims don't make any pictures of the Prophet, peace be upon him, or of any other prophets or important people in Islamic history.[1] Some Muslims are so strict that they won't have their own photos taken!"

"Really?" Nancy looked surprised. "Do people know much about the Prophet, peace be upon him, then?"

"Yes, they do. He was born around 570 in Mecca, but his life was divided between the cities of Mecca and Medina. Today, these cities are in the country of Saudi Arabia."

One of the books was open to a map of ancient Arabia. I showed Nancy where Mecca and Medina were located. "The Prophet, peace be upon him, was born in the house of Banu Hashim. Banu Hashim was just one of the many clans that belonged to the powerful Meccan tribe of Quraysh. He was an orphan—his father, Abdullah, had died before he was born, and his mother, Amina, passed away when he was six years old. He was first raised by his grandfather, Abdul Muttalib, and then his uncle, Abu Talib."

As an adult, the Prophet made a living as a merchant. He didn't know how to read or write, but most people were unlettered in his society at that time. The Arabs were an oral society—they valued beautiful speech and considered poetry to be its highest form.

"It was only when the Prophet, peace be upon him, turned forty that Allah spoke to him and made him a *nabi* (prophet) and a *rasool* (messenger)," I said. "By then, he was married and had children. His wife was Khadija. She was a businesswoman, and Muhammad, peace be upon him, had worked for her in the past. Khadija was fifteen years older than he, but she proposed marriage to him because his character had impressed her."

I told Nancy that the Prophet had a reputation for being honest even before he became a prophet—he was called *al Sadiq al Amin,* which means "truthful and trustworthy."[2] Muslims have great love for the Prophet, and they use the *hadith* to follow his example (*sunnah*). The *hadith* are a collection of teachings of the Prophet that were narrated by other people from his time, sort of like the Gospels in the Bible.

I had brought my copy of the English Quran with me. I asked Nancy to read some of my favorite verses:

Proclaim (or read), in the name of your Lord and Cherisher, who created.
Created man out of a leech-like clot of congealed blood.
Proclaim, and your Lord is Most Bountiful,
He Who taught (the use of) the pen,
Taught man that which he knew not.[3]

I love the story behind these verses. I pulled my chair closer to Nancy.

"These are the first verses of the Quran that Allah communicated to the world. At the time, the Prophet, peace be upon him, was alone in a cave outside of Mecca, where he often spent time by himself. One night in the month of Ramadan, he heard a voice say to him, *'iqra!'* "

I saw Nancy shiver. "I just got goose bumps!" she said. "What does that word mean?"

"It's an Arabic command; it means 'proclaim!' or 'read!' The Prophet, peace be upon him, felt frightened—I've read many books where it says that he felt a pressure on his chest, like he was being squeezed. He didn't know where the voice was coming from. He replied that he didn't know how to read, but the voice simply repeated its command. And then it announced to him the verses that you just read."

Nancy looked frightened, too. "What happened then?" she managed to ask.

"The Prophet, peace be upon him, was so frightened that he ran out of the cave. He thought he was going crazy or that he was being attacked by evil spirits. He was so unhappy that he considered jumping off the mountain and killing himself. He told his wife about the experience when he went home. She became very worried—he was hiding in his room and shivering under a blanket—so she asked a cousin of hers for advice. Khadija's cousin was a *hanif*, someone who believed in the idea of one God, like the Jews and the Christians. He said that the voice her husband had heard belonged to the angel Jibraeel (Gabriel) and that her husband had been chosen by God to be a prophet."

18th-century Christian painting of the Angel Gabriel

The modern city of Medina in Saudi Arabia. Medina is short for Medinat al-Nabi.

"So that's how it all started!" Nancy looked excited.

"Yes," I said. "And he continued to receive revelations from God through Jibraeel for the rest of his life. The Quraysh didn't like the things he was saying. His messages from Allah about justice, equality for all men and women, and worshiping one god challenged their way of life and the way they made money, so they persecuted him and his followers. They even tried to murder him. The people of the oasis of Yathrib gave these early Muslims refuge in their homes, and their city was renamed Medinat al-Nabi, which means the City of the Prophet. This migration to Medinat al-Nabi is called the *hijra,* and the Islamic lunar calendar—AH for *Anno Hegirae*—starts from that year."

I told Nancy about how the Prophet and his *umma* ("community") in Medina struggled with the Arabs from Mecca for ten years. The Meccans eventually gave up the fight and let the Prophet return to Mecca. Ten thousand Muslims marched into Mecca with the Prophet, but their return was peaceful. They forgave the Meccans, but they removed all the idols from the Kaaba. They believed that the shrine had been built by the first man, Aadam (Adam), to worship Allah. Over the next hundred years, the Arab Muslims united under Islam and spread their beliefs through Asia, Africa, and Europe. They ruled many parts of the world. Their most powerful kingdoms were called caliphates, and the last one reigned until the end of World War I.

Mr. Yaseen is a Mongolian Muslim. Mongolia is a Central Asian country located between Russia and China. Muslims make up around three percent of the Mongolian population.

I looked at my watch. It was time for the afternoon prayer. I asked Nancy to gather the books she liked so that the librarian could check them out for us. Her stack was quite high, and it made her look funny. I began to laugh. "Let me help you!" I said.

"Shhh!" said the librarian from his desk. He wore a dark blue suit and a white prayer cap. I knew him; his name is Mr. Yaseen. He is fifty years old and is originally from Mongolia. He means no harm. I smiled at him, and he smiled back at me from behind his thick glasses. *"As-salaam alaikum* ("Peace be upon you")," he said.

"Wa-alaikum as-salaam (And peace be upon you too)," I said.

A Time of Ignorance

Pre-Islamic Arabia was a difficult place to live in. Most of the peninsula is a hot, dry desert; water and vegetation are sparse. Since ancient times, people learned to survive by living in groups, and by the time the Prophet Muhammad was born, Arabia had become a chaotic tribal society. Some Arabs lived in the cities; many still wandered the desert as Bedouins; but they all remained connected to the desert, the home of their nomadic ancestors.

Muslims remember pre-Islamic Arabia as *Jahiliyya* ("The Age of Ignorance").[4] The harshness of the desert seeped into daily life. Disagreements between tribes took many lives and created a huge gap between the rich and the poor. Women and orphans were the weakest members of society. Women did not receive inheritance or an education and had few rights. Many newborn girls were buried alive by their families.

Muhammad's Mecca was a rich city. It made its money from the caravans that traveled through it along the western edge of the peninsula. The city was also an important pilgrimage site—every year people from across Arabia brought the idols they worshiped (and their money) to the Kaaba. Most Arabs worshiped many gods and goddesses, but some chose to believe in the existence of one, all-powerful god. They were inspired by the beliefs of the Jewish and Christian tribes who had a strong presence in Arabia. The religious traditions of the Persians and the Byzantines also greatly influenced Arab society.[5]

Mekka by Hubert Sattler, 1897

19

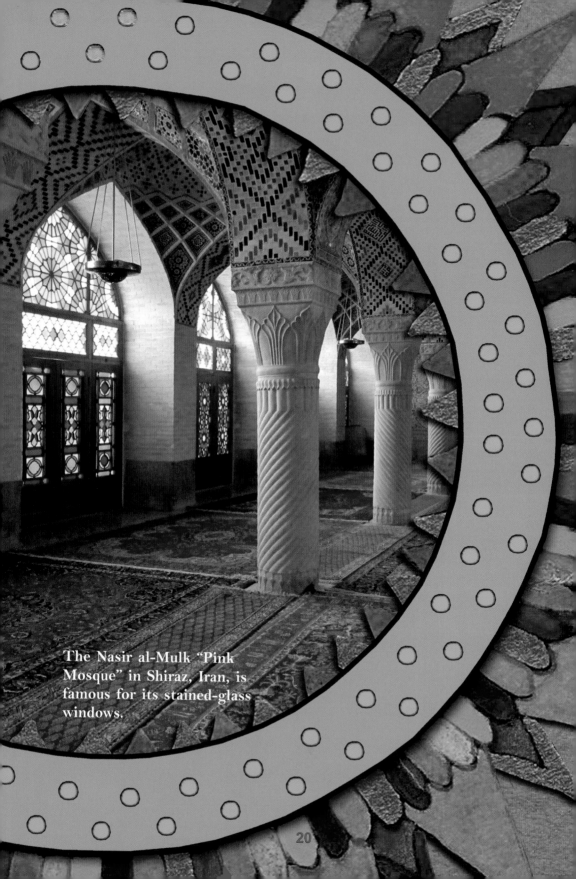

The Nasir al-Mulk "Pink Mosque" in Shiraz, Iran, is famous for its stained-glass windows.

Pillars of Faith

I saw Nancy enter the women's prayer hall from the corner of my eye. I had just finished my afternoon prayers and was making my *dua* (supplication) to Allah. It was a quiet day at the Islamic school—no one else was there. The building had two prayer halls—one for men, one for women.

Nancy was sitting on the carpeted floor by a large bookcase. The bookcase held some *subha* (rosaries), copies of the Quran in Arabic and English, and books about Islam. The carpet had many *sajjada* (prayer rugs) patterned into it. I finished my *dua* and found my way over to her.

"Your *hijaab* is not on too tight, is it?" I said to her. Nancy and I were both wearing colorful scarves around our heads. The prayer hall always has spare ones for women who come to pray.

"Not at all," she said. She showed me some brochures that she was carrying. "I found these while you were praying. We can pass them out in class when we make our presentation."

I picked out one that was titled, *What Is Islam?* The first line of the brochure read:

The word *Islam means "submission to Allah's Divine will," and it comes from the Arabic root for "peace." A Muslim is someone who surrenders his or her troubles to Allah.*

The brochure then talked about Allah. It said that "al-LAH" is Arabic for "the deity," and that He is the same god that Jews and Christians worship.[1] Arabic-speaking Jews and Christians also call God "Allah." The brochure then introduced the *arkan al-Deen* ("pillars of religion").

"What are those?" Nancy asked.

I explained to Nancy that the Five Pillars are the core practices of Islam. In order of importance, they are the *shahada* (belief in Allah and the Prophet), *salaat* (the five daily prayers), *zakaat* (charity), *sawm* (fasting during Ramadan), and *hajj* (the pilgrimage to Mecca).

"The most important thing in Islam is *tawhid,* the idea of one god," I said. "Muslims believe that Allah sent Islam to the world through all his prophets, from Aadam to Isa (Jesus), but the message was always forgotten over time. The Prophet, peace be upon him, was His last messenger, the Seal of the Prophets. Allah can forgive everything except for *shirk,* which is when people make others equal to Him. That is how people convert to Islam, by reciting the *kalima,* which is the declaration of faith."

That is how my parents converted to Islam. They met in college through the Muslim Student Association. My mother had always been curious about Islam. Her grandparents had been Muslims but her parents had grown up under Communism and weren't religious at all. My father had grown up in a Christian Pentecostal family in the United States but had always heard of Islam through his African-American community.

"Do you know the *kalima*?" Nancy asked.

The Kaaba in Mecca. Muslims all over the world turn to face the Kaaba when they pray. The direction towards the Kaaba is called the *qibla*.

"I do," I replied. "This is how it goes: *la ilaaha illalla, Muhammadur rasool ulla*. That means 'I bear witness that there is no god but Allah, and Muhammad is His messenger.'"

"What about the other pillars?" Nancy asked.

"The second pillar is the *salaat,* or the five daily prayers," I said. "These are the prayers of *Fajr, Dhuhr, Asr, Maghrib,* and *Isha* which are performed at dawn, at noon, in the afternoon, at sunset, and at night, respectively. Muslims can pray anywhere—in groups or alone—but many communities build *masjids* (mosques) for community worship. The Friday *Dhuhr* prayer is congregational, and every Muslim man must attend."

"Like in a church where a priest leads the prayer?"

I shook my head.

"Not really. There is no official clergy in Islam, only scholars called *ulama.*[2] Muslims believe that they can pray to Allah directly. The man leading the Friday prayer is usually a respected member of the community. He delivers a sermon called a *khutba* from a pulpit called *minbar.* The pulpit is usually placed next to the *mihrab,* which is a niche in the wall that indicates the direction of the Kaaba in Mecca. Muslims always pray in that direction."

"I've seen Muslims praying before," said Nancy. "What are those movements they make? You were making them also."

"Oh, those movements are repeated a certain number of times as a set. Each set is called a *rakat.*[3] We also recite certain prayers in Arabic while making those movements. And before each prayer, we perform the *wudhu* ablution to purify ourselves."

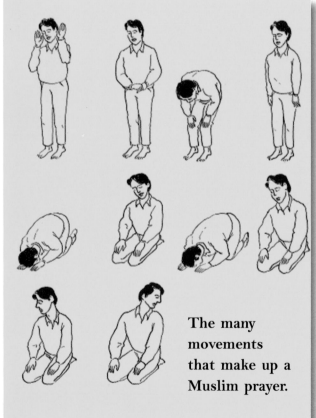

The many movements that make up a Muslim prayer.

I showed Nancy the various movements of a *rakat.* She followed me as I stood up, raised my hands to my ears, and then placed my palms across my chest. I then bent forward and placed my palms on my knees. I sat down and touched the ground with my forehead. Then I sat back up, looked right and left, and put my palms out together in front of me as if I were making a *dua.*

"Layla," she said. "Why are there no pictures of Allah in this prayer hall?"

"Muslims don't make images of Allah," I told her. "We believe that He is beyond human understanding. In fact, we believe that Allah is neither male nor female."[4]

I pointed to a poster on the wall near us. "Those are the ninety-nine names of Allah. Taken together they are called *Asma ul-Husna*, which means 'The Beautiful Names of Allah.' The names are taken from descriptions of Allah found in the Quran."

"They look beautiful. Is that Arabic writing?"

"Yes. The early Muslims avoided making pictures of living things, so their art flourished in the form of religious calligraphy and geometric designs. Many of these designs are very detailed, and almost all revolve around Allah."

"What is the next pillar?"

"Charity. Muslims give away part of their income every year to the needy. Allah says in the Quran that giving charity is a way of purifying one's wealth. The next pillar tells us to fast during the month of Ramadan. Ramadan is the ninth month of the Islamic calendar, and during that time, Muslims do not eat or drink anything between dawn and dusk."

"I still don't know how you do it!" Nancy said.

I finished telling Nancy about the Five Pillars by going over the last one—the pilgrimage to Mecca. Every Muslim tries to make the pilgrimage once in their lifetime. The *hajj* can only be made during the Islamic month of Dhu al-Hijjah, but a lesser pilgrimage called the *umrah* can also be made outside of that time. My parents went on the *hajj* together right after they got married.

"Oh, look," Nancy said. "This brochure also mentions the *Eid* festivals. But why are there two?"

"*Eid* only means 'festival' in Arabic," I said. "*Eid al-Fitr* is the Festival of Breaking the Fast and is celebrated the first three days after Ramadan. *Eid al-Adha* means Festival of Sacrifice and is celebrated on the tenth day of Dhu al-Hijjah."

Muslims across the world remember Ibrahim's (Abraham's) willingness to sacrifice his son Ismail (Ishmael) for Allah (God) during *Eid al-Adha* (the

A sacrificial goat is carried during *Eid al-Adha,* or the Festival of Sacrifice.

Arabs and the Prophet claim descent from Ismail). In the Torah (the Old Testament) and the Bible, it is Isaaq (Isaac) whom Ibrahim chose for the sacrifice. For this *Eid* festival, Muslims offer their own sacrifices in the form of a sheep, cow, or goat, whose meat is divided into thirds and distributed among family, friends, and the less fortunate. Many Muslims also celebrate the Islamic new year (Muharram 1), the birthday of the Prophet (Rabi ul-Awwal 12), and Laylat al-Miraj (Rajab 27). Laylat al-Miraj is the night the Prophet traveled to Jerusalem from Mecca on a mythical white steed called Burraq. In Jerusalem, he rose to Heaven where he visited Allah, the angels, and other prophets.

"All Muslims dress in their best clothes and cook delicious food for the *Eid* festivals," I said. "We visit our friends, and children receive money and other gifts from grown-ups. Everyone always ends up eating too much. The *Eids* and Thanksgiving have that in common!"

A girl steers a boat at a carnival during an *Eid* festival.

The Speech of God

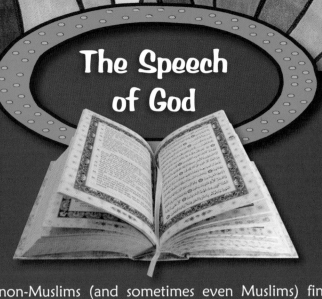

Most non-Muslims (and sometimes even Muslims) find the Quran hard to read; they find its contents contradictory and scattered. This is because the Quran is not structured like a regular book that can be read from start to finish. In fact, the Quran (which means "recitation" in Arabic) did not exist as a book while Muhammad was alive. His revelations were compiled after he died to protect them from change as Islam began to spread beyond Mecca and Medina.

Muslims believe that Allah spoke to the world through Muhammad, which is why the contents of the Quran are in the first person and sound like a monologue. The Quran is divided into 114 chapters called *surahs*, each of which (except one) starts with the phrase, *bismillah-ir-rahman-ir-rahim* ("In the name of God, the Most Gracious, the Most Merciful"). *Surahs* are organized by length in descending order. Each *surah* is made up of verses called *ayah*. Many verses were revealed in response to an immediate need in the Muslim community at the time, and it's important that readers are aware of the context so that they can avoid misunderstanding.[5]

Surahs are most commonly categorized according to where they were revealed. Those that were revealed in Mecca are metaphorical—they contain calls to faith, descriptions of the world and the afterlife, and stories of prophets from Aadam to Isa. The *surahs* from Medina address practical issues that were important to the growing Muslim community. Some of the topics include inheritance, marriage, divorce, and war.

Many Muslims turn to Muslim-owned markets to buy *zabiha* meat.

Famous Faces

It was Sunday afternoon, and my religious classes at the Islamic school had just finished. My father had driven Sinaan, Zoha, and me home. I began looking for Nancy as soon as we entered the house. I found her in the kitchen with my mother.

"Hi, Layla!" Nancy said. "Your mom and I just got back. We went shopping for *Eid.*"

"I took her to the grocery store that is owned by that Afghani family," Mom said as she organized her groceries in the refrigerator. "Nancy, why don't you go spend some time with Layla while I make you some lunch? None of us are going to eat because we're fasting."

Nancy nodded. "Okay, Mrs. Reed, and thank you." I took her hand and we began to walk toward my room. Nancy started telling me how Mom had explained the dietary laws of Muslims to her.[1] Mom had told her how the Quran forbids us from eating certain things, like the meat from pigs, scavengers, carrion, or sick animals. Such things which are not permitted to the Muslims are called *haraam*. Gambling and drinking alcohol are also *haraam*. The things Allah allows us are called *halaal*. Meat such as chicken, beef, or lamb, is always *halaal*, but it must be slaughtered in the name of Allah and completely drained of blood. Meat that is prepared this way is called *zabiha*. Seafood is always *zabiha*.

Nancy and I entered my room, and I saw the books we had checked out from the library yesterday scattered across my bed. Nancy had been studying. Dad's laptop was on the bedside table. We had borrowed it from him for our project.

"I was reading about Islam before I went out with your mom," Nancy said as she opened the laptop. "Did you know that America has had a long history with Islam? Many slaves that were brought to the United States from Africa were Muslim. We hear so much about Islam on the news all the time, but Muslims only form one percent of our population."[2]

Nancy showed me a web site that carried pictures of famous American Muslims. We tried to test ourselves and see how many we could recognize. We knew Muhammad Ali, the boxer, and Malcolm X, the civil rights leader. Both of them used to be part of the Nation of Islam, which was a controversial civil rights group. Muhammad Ali and Malcolm X were its most famous members until they converted to Sunni Islam.

Dr. Mehmet Oz

"Hey, that's Dr. Mehmet Oz," Nancy said. "I've seen him on television with Oprah and on magazine covers. I didn't know he was a Muslim." She searched Dr. Oz on Google and learned that his family was originally from Turkey. We also learned that the name Mehmet is Turkish for Muhammad.

Nancy and I were surprised to discover how many famous Americans practiced Islam—sports stars such as Shaquille O'Neal, Kareem Abdul-Jabbar, Rasheed Wallace, and

Anousheh Ansari

Mike Tyson; comedian Dave Chappelle; and musicians like Ice Cube, Lupe Fiasco, Art Blakey, Mos Def, and Jermaine Jackson.

"That's Michael Jackson's brother!" I exclaimed.

According to the web site, Thomas A. Watson, the man who assisted inventor Alexander Graham Bell, was a Muslim. We also learned about Anousheh Ansari, the first Muslim woman in space. She is originally from Iran.

The web site also had pictures of famous Muslims around the world. We were struck by how beautiful Queen Noor of Jordan was. She was born in America as Lisa Najeeb Halaby but gave up her citizenship and converted to Islam when she married King Hussein of Jordan in 1978.

Nancy pointed to a picture of a thin man with long hair and a beard. "I know him," she said. "That's Cat Stevens. My dad loves his music."

Nancy immediately looked up Cat Stevens on the Internet. She found out that the famous British musician had become a Muslim in 1977. He is now known as Yusuf Islam. Yusuf is what the Muslims call Joseph from the Torah and the Bible.

"Do you know him?" I said as I pointed to a picture of a handsome man. "This is Zinedine Zidane. He is a very famous soccer player from France and is of Algerian descent. I know his face because my brother is crazy about soccer!"

Nancy and I looked up other well-known Muslim people on the Internet. The father of modern medicine, Ibn Sina (known to the West as Avicenna) was a Muslim from present-day Uzbekistan; the Persian al-Razi (Rhazes) founded pediatrics. Another Persian, the mathematician Al-Khwarizmi (Algoritmi), lent his name to the word "algorithm." The philosopher Ibn Rushd (Averroes) was from Cordoba, Spain, and is known in the West for his contributions to secular thought.

Nancy and I had heard of the famous explorer Marco Polo, but we were surprised to learn that a famous Muslim from Morocco called Ibn Battuta had traveled more than him. He even wrote a book called *Rihla* ("Voyage") about the thirty years he spent traveling in Africa, Europe, the Middle East, and Asia. Another famous Muslim is Salah al-Din (Saladin). He was a great Kurdish general whose chivalry inspired respect even in his enemies. Bilal was the first muezzin of Islam. He was an Ethiopian slave who had been set free in the early years of Islam. The Prophet had chosen him to perform the *adhaan* because of his beautiful voice.

Nancy and I played songs on YouTube by the legendary Egyptian singer Umm Kulthum. We watched a trailer for the famous movie *Mohammad: Messenger of God*, which was made by Moustapha Akkad in 1976. Moustapha is another name for the Prophet—it means "chosen one." Akkad was originally from Syria but migrated to the United States where he became famous for producing the *Halloween* movie series. As girls, we were proud to discover that the Muslim countries of Bangladesh and Pakistan had both been led by women—Sheikh Hasina and Benazir Bhutto.

"There are many famous Muslim women in Islamic history," I told Nancy. "Rabia was a famous Sufi saint and poet from Basra, Iraq. Khadija, the first wife of the Prophet, peace be upon him, was the first woman to convert to Islam. The Prophet, peace be upon him, married many women in his lifetime but never while Khadija was alive. When she died, he called it the Year of Sorrow. Khadija had been married more than once before she met the Prophet, peace be upon him, and she had been widowed each time. It said a lot about her that she was able to run a profitable business without a husband in the *Jahiliyya*."

I told Nancy about how the Prophet had all his children—four daughters and also two sons who died in infancy—with Khadija. Their daughter Fatima looms large in Islamic history. She was very close to her father and was the only one of his children through whom their line of descent (the *ahl al-Bayt* or "People of the House") continued. Fatima married Ali, who was the Prophet's cousin and had been the first child to accept Islam. The first man to accept Islam was Abu Bakr. He was the Prophet's friend and would go on to lead the Muslims after the Prophet's death.

The Great Schism

In 632, Muhammad died without naming a successor. Some people believed that the next leader of the Muslims should come from *ahl al-Bayt;* the closest male relative of Muhammad's was Ali. Others wanted to choose a leader according to the ancient Arab tradition of *shura* (consensus).[3] The first four leaders were chosen by consensus and are called the Rightly Guided Caliphs (from *khalifa,* which means "successor"). The third caliph was murdered, and his family fought Ali's family for many years. Ali and his sons were killed, and the descendants of the third caliph went on to establish the Umayyad Caliphate in Damascus.

Another clan from the Quraysh overtook the Umayyads and founded the Abbasid Caliphate in Baghdad. Islam became a formidable world power over the next millennium as many Muslim dynasties ruled across Africa, Europe, and Asia. During that time, different schools (*madhhabs*) of religious jurisprudence (*fiqh*) evolved from the Quran and the *hadith.* These led to the creation of a system of law called *shariah.*

The Muslim World is still divided over who should have succeeded their prophet. Sunni Muslims, who form about 85 percent of the world's Muslim population, believe in the legitimacy of the Rightly Guided Caliphs. Shia Muslims maintain the authority of *ahl al-Bayt.* About 15 percent of all Muslims follow Shia Islam, and every year on Ashura (the tenth day of the Islamic month of Muharram), they mourn the martyrdom of Ali's son, Hussein, at the hands of the Umayyads.[4]

Over the centuries, Islam has experienced many ideological movements within itself. Many people in the West are familiar with the mysticism of Sufi Islam. Other groups like the Baha'i, Druze, Alawi, Alevi, and Ahmadiyya are now considered separate religions by most Muslims.

Best friends Nancy Winters and Layla Reed

Q & A
With Layla and Nancy

Eid Mubarak! A blessed Eid to you! Nancy and I had worked hard all week, and it finally paid off—we were standing at the front of our class and being applauded by our classmates. They loved our presentation. What a wonderful thing to happen to us on *Eid al-Fitr!*

Miss Finney was smiling at us from the back of the classroom. "Thank you so much for the lovely presentation, girls," she said. "And thank you, Layla, for coming in to talk to us today." Miss Finney looked around the room at our classmates. "Layla has taken a holiday from school today, and she will be going home to her family to celebrate *Eid al-Fitr.* Does anyone have any questions or comments for these two before Layla leaves?"

A hand shot up in the first row. It was Emily. She is the most creative person in our class.

Chapter 5

A kaftan

"I love your clothes!" she said. "Your robes look so elegant. They make you look like princesses. What are they called?"

Nancy brightened and stood tall in her turquoise tunic. "Thanks, Emily," she said. "We're wearing kaftans. Layla's mother gave these to us as *Eid* gifts."

"Kaftans are popular in the Middle East and Africa," I added as I adjusted the sequined belt of my pink tunic. "My mother sells a lot of them at her store. You can buy one from there if you like."

Miss Finney spoke up. "Eric has a question," she said as she pointed to the math whiz of our class.

"What is *jihaad?*" he asked. "Is it a holy war against the Christians? I hear people using that word all the time on the news."

I answered Eric's question by first telling him that war can never be holy in Islam. The idea of a holy war came from Europe during the Crusades. The Pope at the time had announced that all Christians who died while fighting the Muslims for control of Jerusalem would become martyrs and go to Heaven.

The Quran only allows Muslims to fight oppression and to stop fighting when the oppression has stopped. Allah says in the Quran that oppression is worse than slaughter. The Quran even lays down rules for fighting. Muslims are not allowed to hurt innocent people, destroy property, or mutilate the bodies of their enemies.

"The word *jihaad* is Arabic for 'struggle,' " I said. "In Islam, *jihaad* implies the struggle to become a better Muslim." I spoke some more about the different kinds of *jihaad* that Muslims can practice to live up to the Islamic ideals of justice, charity, and equality. Being kind to others is *jihaad*. Feeding a stray animal is *jihaad*. Speaking the truth is also *jihaad*. War can be *jihaad* if it is done for a just cause and within the limits given by Allah.[1]

"I have a question," said Elaine. She was new to our school and didn't have many friends. I was so happy that she was joining our conversation.

"Why aren't you wearing veils?" she asked. "Don't all Muslim women have to wear them?"

Nancy and I had discovered many interpretations about that topic in our research. "The Quran asks Muslims—both men and women—to dress modestly," Nancy replied, "but it doesn't mention veils anywhere. Nothing in the Quran asks women to cover their faces."

"Is a veil different from a *hijaab*?" Elaine asked.

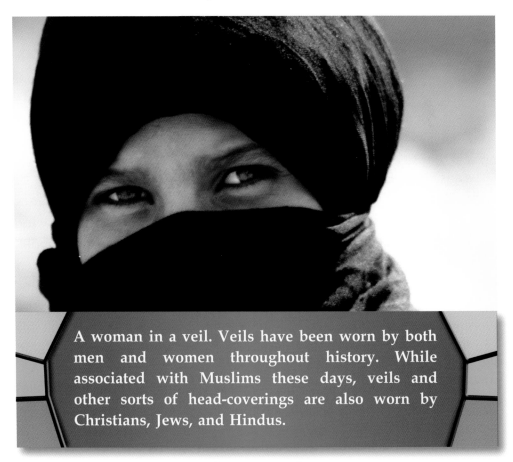

A woman in a veil. Veils have been worn by both men and women throughout history. While associated with Muslims these days, veils and other sorts of head-coverings are also worn by Christians, Jews, and Hindus.

Muslim women wearing *hijaabs*

Nancy and I looked at each other. These were such good questions but so difficult to answer. So much of the way Muslim women dress depends on the culture they are raised in.

"Many Muslim women wear scarves around their hair called *hijaabs*," I said, "but the word itself means 'curtain' or 'screen.' It can also be used to refer to the seclusion of women from the men." I told Elaine about how the Quran only uses the word *hijaab* in reference to the wives of the Prophet, peace be upon him. Allah had asked them to cover themselves when people visited their husband where they lived in Medina in tents. Historians say that Muslim women never wore veils or the modern *hijaab* while the Prophet was alive.[2] They used to mingle freely with men.

"Layla?" I turned to see Avi raising his hand. "Is it true that the Quran tells the Muslims to kill Jewish people?"

I felt so bad about that question. Avi was Jewish. Everyone in the classroom looked at him and then turned to see what Nancy and I would say. Miss Finney looked uncomfortable.

"That's been so misunderstood, Avi," I said. "It's true that the Quran speaks of fighting the Jews in many places, but those verses specifically refer to certain Jewish tribes who were the allies of the Quraysh from Mecca. The Prophet never bore any ill will toward the Jews. In fact, he was inspired by their traditions. During the early years of the *umma,* Muslims prayed in the direction of Jerusalem.[3] They even used to fast with the Jews on Yom Kippur. The Prophet, peace be upon him, had kept the Muslims' congregational prayers on Friday because he did not want to disturb the Jews on the Sabbath."

I told the class about how the Muslims respect the Jews and Christians. They believe that Allah sent His message to every community in the world; they even consider the Jews and Christians to be *ahl al-Kitaab* ("People of the Book"). This particular book is the *umm al-Kitaab* ("Mother Book"), which the Muslims believe is the original, heavenly version of the laws of the Jews, Christians, and Muslims that Allah keeps with Him.[4] The Quran was narrated to the Prophet on Earth from this book.

"The Muslims believe in all the same prophets that the Jews and Christians know," said Nancy. "Even Jesus Christ."

"Really?" said Miss Finney.

"Yes, ma'am," I said. "Except that the Muslims don't believe that he was the son of God. That would be *shirk.* Otherwise the Quran talks about Jesus and his mother Mariam (Mary) with great respect. Even then, the Quran doesn't force Islam on anybody. It says that there can be no compulsion in religion."

I went on to answer many questions in class that day. I was asked if all Muslim men had four wives. The answer is no, that according to the Quran, it is allowed but not recommended. The practice, which was originally meant to place a limit on multiple marriages, is now banned in many Muslim countries. The Quran elevated the status of women in Arabia and gave them many rights where they had none before, including rights of inheritance, marriage, and divorce.

Someone asked me if Muslims worship the Prophet. They don't—that would be *shirk* once again. Muslims love the Prophet and all the prophets before him, but at the end of the day they remember that he was just a human being. Some people refer to the Muslims as Mohammedans, but Muslims don't like that name because it implies that they worship the Prophet, as Christians worship Christ.

Our classmates had a lot more questions for us, but we ran out of time. My mother came to take me home to celebrate *Eid al-Fitr*. My classmates aren't worried though—they know I'll be back. I'll answer all their questions when I return to school tomorrow, *insha Allah* (if Allah wills it)!

At school the most important things we learn can be from each other. "Acquiring knowledge in company for an hour in the night is better than spending the whole night in prayer." (Tirmidhi 256)

The Clash of the Civilizations

Few Americans knew much about Islam until the terrorist attacks in New York City on September 11, 2001. It was much different across the Atlantic Ocean—Europe had known Muslims as immediate neighbors in Africa, Asia, and the Middle East for nearly 1,500 years. For most of that time, people lived in kingdoms that followed a state religion. For instance, the Byzantine Empire in Europe was Christian, the Persian Empire was Zoroastrian, and the Caliphates were Islamic. One's religion was one's citizenship, and religious scriptures were like constitutions.

For most of Islam's history, European rulers struggled with Muslims along their shared borders. The Crusades and European colonialism caused a resentment and suspicion on both sides that lingers on to this day. To Europeans, Muslims were heretics and Muhammad was a dark, frightening figure. In the Scottish language, the word for devil—"Mahound"—is derived from the name of the Prophet.[5] He is portrayed in gory detail in Dante's *Inferno*, with his intestines hanging out of his torn abdomen as he spends eternity in Christian Hell.

Europe's ancient fear of Muslims has gone global in our modern world as Islamophobia. To many Muslims, the United States now represents the Western World that they have mistrusted for so long. This conflict seemed inevitable—Islam is the only major world religion that came into being after Christianity. With the number of Islamic followers growing, it is important that Christians and Muslims learn to respect and honor each other. After all, they both share a common belief in peace and love.

The Star and Crescent, the symbol of Islam

c. 570	Muhammad is born in Mecca.
610	Muhammad has his first revelation.
613	Muhammad preaches in Mecca.
622	Muhammad escapes to Medina and drafts the Constitution of Medina.
630	Meccans accept Islam, and tribal chiefs from all over Arabia swear allegiance to Muhammad.
632	Muhammad dies in Medina.
632–661	Islam expands into the Fertile Crescent, North Africa, Persia, and Byzantium.
c. 650	The Quran is compiled.
661–750	Islam spreads into Africa, Asia, and Europe.
750–1258	Islam spreads into India and China.
768	Muhammad Ibn Ishaq writes the first written biography of Muhammad.
800s	The *hadith* are compiled.
934–1062	The Buyid Dynasty rules western Iran, Iraq, and Mesopotamia.
970	The al-Azhar University is founded in Cairo.
977–1186	The Ghaznavid Dynasty rules Khurasan, Afghanistan, and northern India.
1095–1453	The period of the Christian Crusades.
1281–1924	The Ottoman Empire is founded in present-day Turkey.
1501–1723	The Safavid Empire rules in Persia.
1520–1857	The Mughal Dynasty rules India. The Taj Mahal is built in Agra in 1653.
1870–1924	Arab Muslims migrate to the United States.
1919	One of the first mosques in America is established in Detroit, Michigan.
1930	The Nation of Islam in founded in the United States.
1938	Oil is discovered in the Middle East.
1945	The Arab League is formed.
1945–1970	Mass migrations from Asia and Africa bring Islam to the West.
1992	The demolition of a mosque in Ayodhya, India, by a Hindu mob leads to violence across the country.
2001	Al-Qaeda attacks New York and Washington, DC.
2003	Shirin Ebadi becomes the first Muslim woman to win the Nobel Peace Prize.
2007	Keith Ellison becomes the first Muslim to be elected to the United States Congress.
2011	Al-Qaeda founder Osama bin Laden is killed by American forces in Pakistan.
2013	Chechen Muslims are suspected of bombing runners during the Boston Marathon.

Chapter 1 Ramadan with the Reeds

1. Abdullah Yusuf Ali, *The Meanings of the Illustrious Quran* (Philadelphia: Alminar Books, 1997), p. 584.
2. Paul Grieve, *A Brief Guide to Islam—History, Faith, and Politics: The Complete Introduction* (New York: Carroll and Graf Publishers, 2006), p. 112.
3. Drew Desilver, "World's Muslim Population More Widespread Than You Might Think," *Pew Research Center*, June 7, 2013, http://www.pewresearch.org/fact-tank/2013/06/07/worlds-muslim-population-more-widespread-than-you-might-think/
4. Ibid.
5. Ibid.

Chapter 2 A Prophet from Mecca

1. John Bowker, *World Religions* (New York: DK Publishing, 2003), pp. 180-181.
2. Annemarie Schimmel, *Islam—An Introduction* (Albany, NY: State University of New York Press, 1992), p. 11.
3. Abdullah Yusuf Ali, *The Meanings of the Illustrious Quran* (Philadelphia: Alminar Books, 1997), p. 583.
4. Justin Wintle, *History of Islam* (London: Rough Guides Limited, 2003), p. 39.
5. 5. Schimmel, pp. 7–9.

Chapter 3 Pillars of Faith

1. Reza Aslan, *No god but God* (London: Arrow Books, 2005), p. 6.
2. Paul Grieve, *A Brief Guide to Islam—History, Faith, and Politics: The Complete Introduction* (New York: Carroll and Graf Publishers, 2006), p. 229.
3. Annemarie Schimmel, *Islam—An Introduction* (Albany, NY: State University of New York Press, 1992), pp. 39–42.
4. Mary Margaret Funk, *Islam Is . . .* (New York: Lantern Books, 2003), pp. 35–37.
5. Justin Wintle, *History of Islam* (London: Rough Guides Limited, 2003), pp. 12–13.

Chapter 4 Famous Faces

1. Paul Grieve, *A Brief Guide to Islam—History, Faith, and Politics: The Complete Introduction* (New York: Carroll and Graf Publishers, 2006), pp. 246–250.
2. Religion & Public Life: Muslims, http://www.pewforum.org/global-religious-landscape-muslim.aspx
3. Reza Aslan, *No god but God* (London: Arrow Books, 2005), p. 112.
4. Ibid., p. 244.

Chapter 5 Q & A with Layla and Nancy

1. John Bowker, *World Religions* (New York: DK Publishing, 2003), pp. 184–185.
2. Reza Aslan, *No god but God* (London: Arrow Books, 2005), pp. 65–66.
3. Paul Grieve, *A Brief Guide to Islam—History, Faith, and Politics: The Complete Introduction* (New York: Carroll and Graf Publishers, 2006), pp. 8–17.
4. Bowker, pp. 182–183.
5. Annemarie Schimmel, *Islam—An Introduction* (Albany, NY: State University of New York Press, 1992), pp. 1–6.

Books

Ali-Karamali, Sumbul. *Growing Up Muslim—Understanding the Beliefs and Practices of Islam.* New York: Delacorte Books for Young Readers, 2012.

Demi. *Muhammad.* New York: Margaret K. McElderry Books, 2003.

Khan, Michelle. *The Hijab Boutique.* Leicestershire, UK: The Islamic Foundation, 2011.

Khan, Saniyasnain. *My First Quran Storybook—The Best Treasured Stories from the   Quran.* New Delhi: Goodword Books, 2009.

Wolf, Bernard. *Coming to America—A Muslim Family's Story.* New York: Lee & Low Books, 2003.

Woodhall, Ruth, and Shahada Sharelle Abdul Haqq. *Stories of the Prophets in the Holy Quran.* Somerset, NJ: Tughra Books, 2008.

Works Consulted

Ali, Abdullah Yusuf. *The Meanings of the Illustrious Quran.* Philadelphia: Alminar Books, 1997.

Aslan, Reza. *No god but God.* London: Arrow Books, 2005.

Bowker, John. *World Religions.* New York: DK Publishing, 2003.

Funk, Mary Margaret. *Islam Is . . .* New York: Lantern Books, 2003.

Grieve, Paul. *A Brief Guide to Islam—History, Faith, and Politics: The Complete Introduction.* New York: Carroll and Graf Publishers, 2006.

Pew Forum. www.pewforum.org/2012/12/18/ global-religious-landscape-muslim/

Schimmel, Annemarie. *Islam—An Introduction.* Albany, NY: State University of New York Press, 1992.

Wintle, Justin. *History of Islam.* London: Rough Guides Limited, 2003.

Internet

BBC Religions: Islam

http://www.bbc.co.uk/religion/religions/islam/

Discover the Muslim Heritage in Our World: 1,001 Inventions

http://www.1001inventions.com/

Hafiz, Yasmine. "Nasir al-Mulk 'Pink Mosque' Of Iran Is Like Stepping into a Kaleidoscope." The Huffington Post, March 15, 2014. http://www.huffingtonpost.com/2014/03/15/nasir-al-mulk-pink-mosque_n_4959362.html

Islamic Society of North America

http://www.isna.net/

The Qur'an

http://quran.com/

Religion & Public Life: Muslims

http://www.pewforum.org/global-religious-landscape-muslim.aspx

ablution (AB-loo-shun)—A ritual washing or cleansing of the body.

algorithm (AL-guh-rhythm)—A sequence of steps programmed in a computer to solve a specific problem.

calligraphy (kuh-LIH-gruh-fee)—The art of fine handwriting.

caravan (KARE-uh-van)—A group of travelers journeying together for safety in hostile territory.

carrion (KARE-ee-in)—Dead and decaying flesh.

clergy (KLER-jee)—The body of people ordained for religious service.

congeal (KUN-jeel)—To solidify by freezing.

jurisprudence (jur-iss-PROO-dinse)—The philosophy or science of law.

martyrdom (MAR-tur-dum)—Death that is imposed because of one's faith or cause.

muezzin (myoo-EH-zin)—A crier who calls Muslims to prayer five times a day from the minaret of a mosque.

oasis (oh-AY-sys)—A fertile or green spot in a desert, often near a body of water.

pediatrics (pee-dee-AT-rix)—The branch of medicine that deals with the care of infants and children.

peninsula (peh-NIN-soo-la)—A large mass of land projecting into a body of water.

prophet (PRAH-fit)—A person who speaks for God or a deity, or by divine inspiration.

pulpit—A raised platform that gives prominence to the person on it.

scavenger (SKAV-in-jer)—An animal that feeds on dead organisms.

secular (SEK-yoo-lur)—Not concerned with or related to religion.

supplication (sup-lih-KAY-shun)—A prayer asking God's help as part of a religious service.

terrorist (TAYR-uh-rist)—A radical person who uses terror as a political weapon.

Khadija Ejaz is an internationally published and translated poet and author. She was born in Lucknow, India, raised in Muscat, Oman, and has also lived in Toronto, Canada, and New Delhi, India. Ejaz now lives in the United States, where she earned her undergraduate and graduate degrees in information technology. She has worked in broadcast journalism at New Delhi Television and dabbles in filmmaking and photography. To learn more about Ejaz, visit her web site at http://khadijaejaz.netfirms.com.